For Freya

*This book is dedicated to the disappearing
apple orchards of England*

With thanks to Viva

Copyright © 1996 by Sandy Nightingale

The rights of Sandy Nightingale to be identified as the author and illustrator of this work have been
asserted by her in accordance with the Copyright, Designs and Patents Act, 1988.
First published in Great Britain in 1996 by Andersen Press Ltd., 20 Vauxhall Bridge Road,
London SW1V 2SA. Published in Australia by Random House Australia Pty., 20 Alfred Street,
Milsons Point, Sydney, NSW 2061. All rights reserved. Colour separated in Switzerland by
Photolitho AG, Offsetreproduktionen, Gossau, Zürich. Printed and bound in Italy by Grafiche
AZ, Verona.

10   9   8   7   6   5   4   3   2   1

British Library Cataloguing in Publication Data available.
ISBN 0 86264 622 7

This book has been printed on acid-free paper

CIDER APPLES

Written and Illustrated by
Sandy Nightingale

Andersen Press • London

IT WAS just before midnight on New Year's Eve. Holly couldn't sleep. She could hear her grandparents talking in the sitting room below.

"There's nothing we can do." That was Grandpa's voice. "The apple trees are dying and if they die we will have to sell the cottage."

"Something may turn up," said Grandma.

"I don't think so," said Grandpa. "We can't manage without the cider apple money."

Holly caught her breath. Grandpa's grandpa had lived in this cottage and Holly loved coming to stay here.

After Grandpa had gone to bed, Holly ran downstairs.

"Oh, Grandma," she cried, "you can't sell Apple Tree Cottage."

"Cheer up," smiled Grandma. "I haven't given up hope. New Year is such a magical time, anything might happen. Listen!"

Just then, the clock on the mantelpiece chimed the first stroke of midnight.

"At last!" purred a strange musical voice. It was Magic the cat. Holly and Grandma stared in amazement.

"Come on!" said Magic. "There's no time to lose."

He looked at their wondering faces.

"Animals can speak in the moments between the old year and the new," he explained. "Shadow has something important to tell you."

In his stable, Shadow tossed his mane.

"When I was a foal," he said, "I heard a strange tale about the Apple Tree Man, who looks after orchards. Listen carefully. This is what you must do if you want to save the apple trees..."

"Take the last drop of last year's cider and put it into a big pan with some cinnamon and honey. Heat it gently. Pour the warm cider over the roots of the oldest tree in the orchard and see what happens. But hurry. The magic only works tonight."

Holly and Grandma did exactly as Shadow had told them.

As soon as the cider soaked into the frozen ground a ring of toadstools sprang out of the snow.

"Stand back," whispered Grandma. "You must never step inside a fairy ring."

For a moment everything was silent.

Then, suddenly, there appeared from the roots of the tree a stream of fairies, laughing, singing and dancing. They poured into the orchard, up into the branches, and tumbled into the air. Some played musical instruments; strumming, piping and beating time as they whirled around.

Holly watched with shining eyes. She had never seen anything so beautiful.

A peculiar old man was grinning at them from the tree. He clapped his long, bony hands and the fairies were quiet.

"I know why you have called me here," he laughed. "But I can only heal these trees if Holly will promise to plant all the pips from the first apple she picks."

He looked at Holly. "Will you promise me this?"

"Oh, I promise," cried Holly, eagerly.

The Apple Tree Man nodded his head and clapped his hands again. The fairy music became louder and louder as the troupe of fairies moved through the orchard dancing around every tree.

Then, just as suddenly as they had come, the fairies disappeared.

Holly and Grandma gazed around the quiet orchard.   Everything was still.

"Let's get you tucked up in bed," said Grandma.   "It's freezing.   We've done what we can.   Now we must wait."

Holly climbed into her cosy bed and fell asleep at once.   Outside, the snow began to fall silently.

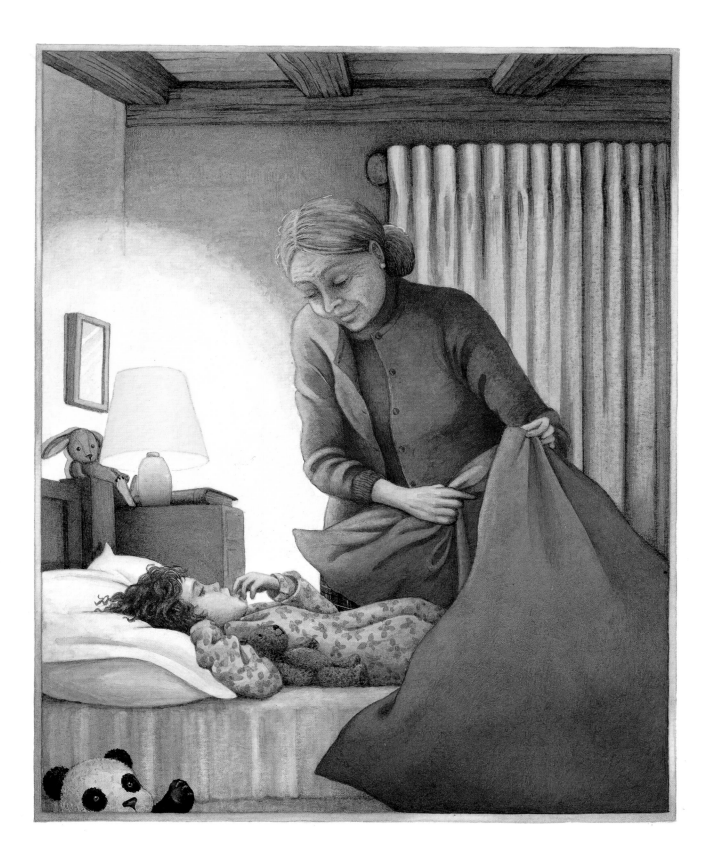

A robin singing outside her window woke Holly. She immediately thought of the orchard. She ran to the window and looked out at the snowy world. Did the trees look any different?

Grandma woke with the wintry sunshine streaming into the bedroom. She stretched and yawned.

"I've had such a funny dream," she said. Then she heard Holly's voice calling excitedly.

"Grandma, Grandpa, come and look. Come and see!"

Out in the orchard, under a covering of snow, the oldest tree was laden with beautiful, juicy apples. Grandpa stared in wonder.

"It's a miracle," he said. "Our house is saved."

Holly ran to the tree.

Shadow deserves an apple, she thought.

"Thank you, Apple Tree Man," she whispered. "I won't forget my promise." And she reached up to pick her first apple.